Cambridge Discovery Education™

► INTERACTIVE READERS

Series editor: Bob Hastings

AROUND JAPAN IN THREE DAYS

A1+

Simon Beaver

CAMBRIDGE
UNIVERSITY PRESS

●DISCOVERY
EDUCATION™

CAMBRIDGE UNIVERSITY PRESS
Cambridge, New York, Melbourne, Madrid, Cape Town,
Singapore, São Paulo, Delhi, Mexico City

Cambridge University Press
32 Avenue of the Americas, New York, NY 10013-2473, USA

www.cambridge.org
Information on this title: www.cambridge.org/9781107661332

First published 2014
Reprinted 2014

Printed in Hong Kong, China, by Golden Cup Printing Company Limited

A catalog record for this publication is available from the British Library.

Library of Congress Cataloging-in-Publication Data

Beaver, Simon.
  Around Japan in three days / Simon Beaver.
     pages cm. -- (Cambridge discovery interactive readers)
  ISBN 978-1-107-66133-2 (pbk. : alk. paper)
  1. Japan--Juvenile literature. 2. English language--Textbooks for foreign speakers. 3. Readers
(Elementary) I. Title.

DS806.B39 2014
952--dc23

                                      2013016882

ISBN 978-1-107-66133-2

Additional resources for this publication at www.cambridge.org

Cambridge University Press has no responsibility for the persistence or
accuracy of URLs for external or third-party Internet Web sites referred to in
this publication and does not guarantee that any content on such Web sites is,
or will remain, accurate or appropriate.

Layout services, art direction, book design, and photo research: Q2ABillSMITH GROUP
Editorial services: Hyphen S.A.
Audio production: CityVox, New York
Video production: Q2ABillSMITH GROUP

Contents

Before You Read:
Get Ready!

Japan is a great country. Learn about some of the things that you can do there.

Words to Know

Complete the sentences with the correct words.

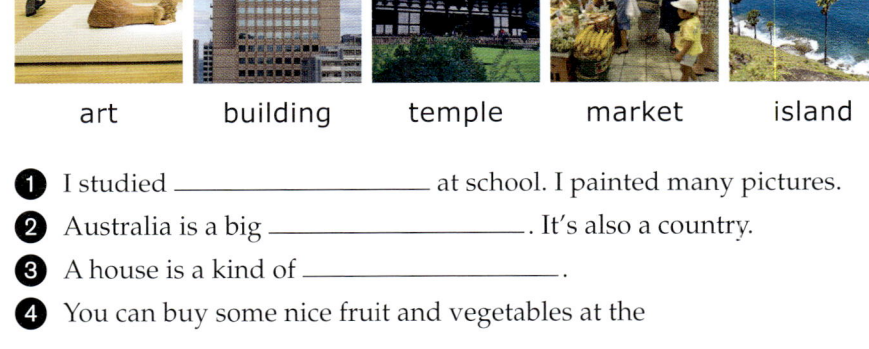

art   building   temple   market   island

1 I studied _____ at school. I painted many pictures.

2 Australia is a big _____. It's also a country.

3 A house is a kind of _____.

4 You can buy some nice fruit and vegetables at the _____.

5 A _____ is a special building for a religion.

Words to Know

Read the paragraph. Then complete the sentences with the correct highlighted words.

I'm going to tell you a story. I started to drive home yesterday, but then a cat ran in front of my car. It was very dangerous. I stopped and got out of the car, but the cat did not move. When I went near it, it climbed on top of the car like the car was a mountain! Because there was a cat on my car, I couldn't go home. So I talked to the cat. There were people everywhere. They all stopped to watch me. I asked the cat to go many times, and even sang it a traditional song from my mother's country. The cat didn't listen to me. It went to sleep. The people loved the cat.

1. I often _____ the tall tree near my house when I was a child.

2. There are a lot of fun places to shop in the city. There are stores _____ .

3. I like restaurants where they serve food from one culture and also play _____ , old music.

4. The TV was in the wrong place. I had to _____ it.

5. He drives very fast. I think it's very _____ to do that.

6. You can see a tall _____ from our school. It's very beautiful in the late afternoon.

?

PREPARE

This book is about Japan. What do you know about Japan? Where is it? How many islands does it have? How many people live there? What's the name of the biggest city? Read on to check your answers.

5

CHAPTER 1

A Very Different Country

JAPAN IS A COUNTRY OF THOUSANDS OF ISLANDS! JAPAN'S MOST IMPORTANT CITIES ARE ON ITS BIGGEST ISLAND: HONSHU. THE JAPANESE MAKE A LOT OF THINGS: CARS, BIKES, TRAINS, BOATS, COMPUTERS, TELEVISIONS, RADIOS, CAMERAS, AND GUITARS.

People

Japan has 127 million people. They live longer than people in almost any other country! Some people think this is because they eat well. Japanese food is famous **everywhere** in the world. Most people know sushi, which is usually made with rice and raw[1] fish.

[1] **raw:** not cooked

Art

Japan's music, **art**, and buildings are very different from those in other countries. One kind of Japanese art is manga: books of pictures that tell stories. The Japanese language does not use letters like A, B, and C in English to make words. It uses pictures called logograms. You can buy manga in many different languages. You don't have to read Japanese!

Tourists

People like to visit Japan on vacation. About nine million tourists[2] come to Japan every year. There's a lot to see and do there!

....

[2] **tourist:** a visitor on vacation

?

EVALUATE

Do you have things that were made in Japan? What are they? Why do people buy things that are made in Japan?

The Tsukiji fish market

CHAPTER 2

Day 1: Visit Tokyo

TOKYO IS THE BIGGEST CITY IN JAPAN. IT'S A VERY EXCITING PLACE. THERE'S SO MUCH TO DO! MARKETS, RESTAURANTS, SHOPPING, THEATER…

Market

Before lunch, do you want to see where the food comes from? Why not visit the Tsukiji fish **market**? The Japanese love fish, and Tsukiji is the biggest fish market in the world!

You can go there really early. It usually opens at 3 a.m.! That's when fish arrives from all over the world. It gets very busy between 5 and 8 a.m.

There's every kind of fish at the market. You see big, small, colorful, and unusual fish. And there are auctions. In an auction, you and other people want to buy some fish. You say how much you are ready to pay. Other people do the same. If you can pay the most, you get the fish.

Video Quest

Traveling in Tokyo

Watch the video about Tokyo. How many people live there? What kinds of transportation[3] do they use to go to work?

[3]**transportation:** trains, buses, planes, and cars are all kinds of transportation

Food

Food in Tokyo is great. The Japanese love a meal called ramen noodles – a kind of pasta, like spaghetti. People often wait a long time outside a good noodle restaurant!

Or try a sushi restaurant. At a sushi restaurant, you sit and the table **moves**! The table carries plates of rice and fish in front of you. When you see something good, you can take it!

Theater

After dinner, you can see **traditional** shows at the Akasaka Act Theater. The actors speak Japanese, but you can listen to the words in English.

Shopping

Why not go to the Ginza part of Tokyo? In 1612 there was a factory called Ginza here. The factory made different kinds of money. It was a mint.

Now the Ginza makes money in a different way. Some of the world's best clothing stores, restaurants, and cafés are in the Ginza. If you like art and enjoy seeing pictures and photos, there are fantastic art galleries,[4] too.

On weekends, there are no cars on Chuo-dori street. There are lots of people, and you can listen to great street music there!

[4] **gallery:** a place where you can see and buy art

EVALUATE

Why do you think some of the world's best stores are in Tokyo?

CHAPTER 3

Day 2: A Bullet Train to Kyoto

JAPAN'S BULLET TRAINS ARE FAMOUS. ENJOY THE RIDE TO OLD KYOTO – JAPAN'S MOST IMPORTANT CITY FOR HUNDREDS OF YEARS.

Catch the Bullet Train

Japan was the first country to have these very fast trains. The first bullet train started in 1964. It traveled between Japan's biggest cities, Tokyo and Osaka. Today, there are bullet trains between all the biggest cities on the islands of Honshu and Kyushu. Why not take one to Kyoto? Kyoto was the most important city in Japan until 1868.

The famous Japanese bullet trains

When you get on the bullet train, you see that it's very clean inside. And your seat is very comfortable!

The train goes faster and faster. You look out of the window. Everything goes past so quickly! In the end, you are traveling at 300 kilometers an hour!

A waiter comes and you get some tea. Then the train stops. Not a minute late! Did it really get to Kyoto so fast? Japanese trains are fantastic!

?

UNDERSTAND

Which cities did the first bullet train travel between? How fast does a bullet train go today?

In Kyoto

Now you're in Kyoto, and you need a place to stay. If you have a lot of money, stay in a *ryokan*, a beautiful traditional Japanese hotel. A night in a ryokan is something to remember! But if you have less money, stay in a *minshuku*. Minshukus are not as good as ryokans, but they are nice.

It's time to visit Kyoto! Go to the part of the city called Higashiyama, with its beautiful **temples** and parks. There's a zoo, too.

Kinkaku-ji Temple, Kyoto

Next, visit Kinkaku-ji Temple. In 1400, it was the house of an important man. When he died, his son made a temple there. The building is above a big pool of water. You can take a beautiful photo of the temple in the water.

Enjoy

Are you hungry now? The Pontocho part of the city has many restaurants and teahouses. It also has many geisha houses and sometimes real geisha shows.

Geishas

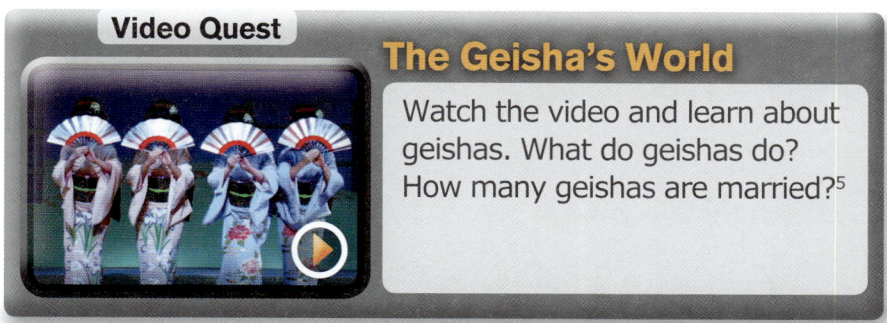

Video Quest

The Geisha's World

Watch the video and learn about geishas. What do geishas do? How many geishas are married?[5]

....

[5]**be married:** have a husband or wife

CHAPTER 4

Day 3: Climbing Mount Fuji

YOU HAVE ONE LAST, EXCITING THING TO DO IN JAPAN. YOU'RE GOING TO CLIMB THE HIGHEST MOUNTAIN IN THE COUNTRY!

Get Ready

Start your morning with a traditional Japanese breakfast. The Japanese eat rice and soup for breakfast. They also eat eggs, fish, and vegetables.

Next, take a look at Kyoto's fantastic train station. It's one of the biggest buildings in Japan. Inside there's a big store, a hotel, and a movie theater. Some people don't like the station because it's a new kind of building and not traditional.

?
ANALYZE
A lot of people climb Mount Fuji. What other mountains do people climb? Why do you think people climb mountains?

Now it's time to take the train from Kyoto to Shin-Fuji, near Mount Fuji. The train is fast – you're there in only two and a half hours.

Look at beautiful Mount Fuji. Mount Fuji is a volcano,[6] but it isn't usually dangerous. The last time the volcano erupted[7] was in 1707 – more than 300 years ago. But it may erupt again soon!

[6]**volcano** (noun): a mountain with a hole in it that hot rock can come out of.
[7]**erupt:** when a volcano gets very, very hot inside, and the hot rock on the inside comes out

Climb

You can only climb Mount Fuji in July and August. The weather is too dangerous in other months.

First, take the bus from Shin-Fuji to Mount Fuji. In two hours, it takes you to the Fujinomiya mountain station. Now you are 2,400 meters up. Fuji is 3,776 meters high. That's not too bad, but climbing on **trails** can be dangerous. You must have the right shoes, clothes, and food.

On the trail, there are hotels called huts where you can sleep. Call one before you leave. Ask them to have a meal and a bed ready for you. After climbing to the hotel, you are going to want to eat and sleep.

There are four different trails up Mount Fuji.

When you wake up, you have to climb in the dark to get to the top at 4:30 a.m. Then you can watch the sun come up. It's really beautiful. Remember to take your camera!

Some people don't sleep on the mountain. They climb it and come back down the same day. Other people sleep there because it's easier to climb to the top early to see the sun come up.

Video Quest

Hot Springs

Watch the video and learn about Japan's hot water pools, called hot springs. What kind of animal likes hot springs?

CHAPTER 5

What Do You Think?

So now you know, there are a lot of things to see and do in Japan. You read about the big fish market in Tokyo, sushi and other Japanese food, the stores and art galleries of the Ginza, traditional Japanese theater, hotels in cities and on a mountain, very fast, clean trains, big train stations, and beautiful old temples.

What do you think are the best things about Japan? Is there anything you don't like so much? Would you like to have some things from Japan in your country? Would you like to live in Tokyo?

The Japanese often enjoy very traditional things. What are the most important traditional things in your country? They can be food, buildings, clothes, or other things. Which of them do you like the most?

If you go to Japan on vacation, which three things in this book do you most want to do? Why did you choose those things? If you know Japan, which of the things in this book did you see or do? Did you enjoy them?

After You Read

Read the sentences and choose Ⓐ (True) or Ⓑ (False). If the book does not tell you, choose Ⓒ (Doesn't say).

1 People usually make sushi with rice and fish.

Ⓐ True
Ⓑ False
Ⓒ Doesn't say

2 You can find 1,000 different kinds of fish in Tsukiji market.

Ⓐ True
Ⓑ False
Ⓒ Doesn't say

3 The Ginza is a great place to go shopping.

Ⓐ True
Ⓑ False
Ⓒ Doesn't say

4 Bullet trains travel at 400 kilometers an hour.

Ⓐ True
Ⓑ False
Ⓒ Doesn't say

5 A ryokan is a beautiful traditional Japanese theater.

Ⓐ True
Ⓑ False
Ⓒ Doesn't say

6 There's a bookstore in Kyoto Station.

Ⓐ True
Ⓑ False
Ⓒ Doesn't say

7 Mount Fuji is 2,400 meters tall.

   Ⓐ True

   Ⓑ False

   Ⓒ Doesn't say

8 The best time to get to the top of Mount Fuji is 4:30 a.m.

   Ⓐ True

   Ⓑ False

   Ⓒ Doesn't say

Complete the Chart

Write down the names of three of the places in this book. Say what you can do there. Then say why you would (or would not) like to do it.

Place	What can you do there?	Would you like to do this?

Complete the Text

Write one word in each space.

Fuji is the name of a big **1** ———————————. You can only **2** ——————————— it in July or August, because in other months, the weather is too **3** ———————————. The **4** ——————————— on Mount Fuji are called huts.

Answer Key

Words to Know, page 4

1 art **2** island **3** building **4** market **5** temple

Words to Know, page 5

1 climbed **2** everywhere **3** traditional **4** move
5 dangerous **6** mountain

Prepare, page 5

Answers will vary.

Evaluate, page 7

Answers will vary.

Video Quest, page 9

35 million people. Taxis, trains, planes.

Evaluate, page 11

Answers will vary.

Understand, page 13

The first bullet train traveled between Tokyo and Osaka.
Today, bullet trains travel at 300 kilometers an hour.

Video Quest, page 15

Geishas dance and make music. No geishas are married.

Analyze, page 17

Answers will vary.

Video Quest, page 19

The snow monkey likes hot springs.

True or False, page 22

1 A **2** C **3** A **4** B **5** B **6** C **7** B **8** A

Complete the Chart, page 23

Answers will vary.

Complete the Text, page 23

1 mountain / volcano **2** climb **3** dangerous **4** hotels